Would you like to eat

Soft Fluffy Idlis?

Written by Radhika Suri

Illustrated by Upasana Chadha

Art Direction by Surbhi Bhadani

Meet the gang

from the 'Yummylicious Make-Belief' series

Kai

Pai

Gobi

www.taleswithradhika.com

tales with radhika

I love Idlis!
Idlis?
Idlis?

Idlis?

They are white like the jasmine,
They are soft and fluffy like the clouds...
They taste so light and tangy... yummy!

Let us make idlis Ajji!
Yummy!

Take some lentil,
take some rice,
and pour some water -POUR, POUR, POUR!

Soak it for 8 hours
-SOAK, SOAK, SOAK!
Now let us grind it
-GRIND, GRIND, GRIND!
WRRRRR....

Let us put the dish with the batter where the sun will keep it warm.
and wait for it to... RISE, RISE, RISE!
Has it risen?
NO! NO!

There is a cloud in front of the sun!
How will our idli batter rise?
Has it risen?
NEWS
NO! NO!

Let us take it inside the house.
Let us hug it -HUG, HUG, HUG!
Its not rising!

Let us wrap it up in our woolens to keep it cozy and warm and WAIT, WAIT, WAIT!

After a few hours !
1. 2. 3. 4. 5. 6. 7. 8.
Something is peeking out- WHITE, WHITE, WHITE!

It's RISEN!
Ajji, quick!
The batter is ready, make
us some idlis.

I will make you idlis served with sambhar and chutney.

I cannot stop eating these soft idlis!

Soft, tangy so delicious, Ajji!
Yummy !

Ajji, we have eaten so many idlis.
Guess how many we ate Ajji?

6? 8? 10?

Decorate the Idlis with Your Favorite Herbs and Vegetables.

What All Can an Idli Be?

A cuddly pillow

A small fluffy cloud

A clock with curry leaf arms

A moon

Let us Imagine Even More!

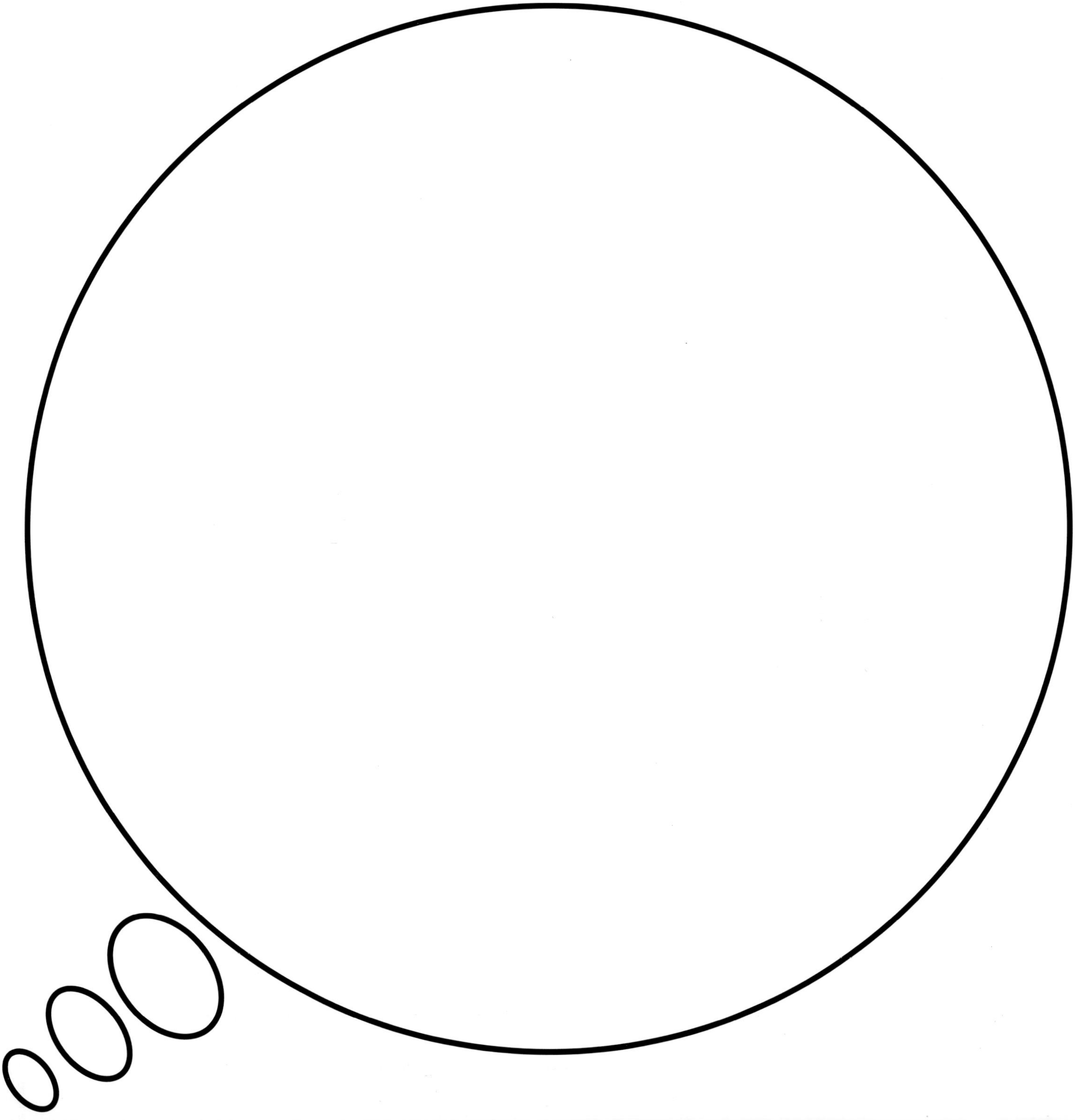

We have an Idli tummy!

Guess How Many Idlis we Ate?

Kai -	Pai -	Gobi -